The Columbian presents

Clark County

VOLUME II ~ 1950 - 1999

Acknowledgments

The skill and ability of photographers listed here made this publication possible.

The Columbian:

Bob Beck
Reid Blackburn
Kim Blau
Geoff Borden
Tom Boyd
Rick Browne
Milan Chuckovich
Gordon Clark
Jeremiah Coughlan

John Ford
Barbara Gundle
Cheryl Haselhorst
Walt Hicks
Beth Campbell Hovee
Alice Jackson
Casey Madison
Janet Mathews
Scott Miller

Ted Olsen
Dave Olson
Steve Small
Thomas Ryll
David Tinney
Ted Van Arsdol
Troy Wayrynen
Lisa Wright

Additional photos were provided by:

Ackroyd Photography Inc.
Art Commercial Studios
AP
Sherry Angel
BPA
Bruno Studio
Delano Studios & Aerial Surveys

Sam Feldman
Crista Jeremiason
Fred Milkie
Lowell Moore
Parkers
James Ryan
Stuart Thurlkill

Vanity Fair
Washington State Department of Transportation
Werner Lenggenhager
Walters Studio

Copyright© 2000 • ISBN: 1-891395-55-6

Published by Pediment Publishing, a division of The Pediment Group, Inc. www.pediment.com

Table of Contents

Foreword

The daily process of reporting the news for the communities that make up Clark County rarely provides the opportunity to step back and look at all that has happened leading to where we are today. This pictorial history is intended to provide you with just that opportunity: to look at the highlights of the last 50 years and begin to appreciate the challenges, accomplishments, celebrations and tragedies that helped to make Clark County, Washington the vibrant community we know it to be today.

The response to *Clark County - The Early Years* covering the earliest days of the community through 1949 was overwhelming. Selling out of our initial pressrun, we've sold over 5,000 copies and are nearly sold out of our second printing.

We are particularly proud of this volume given that it is comprised mostly of photographs taken by photographers of *The Columbian*, each of whom is identified on page 2 and to whom we are extremely grateful. The advent of quality photo reproduction enabled newspapers to complement the reporting each day in a manner that line art and words alone could never accomplish.

We relied heavily on the assistance of local historian Ted Van Arsdol to provide the necessary research. Without Ted's tenacity and passion for the local history we would never be able to present a book with the quality we believe we're providing with this collection. A number of dedicated folks at *The Columbian* were also instrumental in bringing the project to life. Our thanks go to Diane Gibson, Cynthia Dailey, Linda Lutes and Rick Browne.

Chronicling the events of our community is our passion and we strive to exceed our reader's expectation every day through the pages of *The Columbian*. We believe the same passion will be evident in *Clark County – Volume II 1950-1999*.

Scott Campbell
Publisher, *The Columbian*

The 1950s

At the start of the 1950s decade, Clark County still was feeling some of the economic letdown from the end of World War II. The Kaiser shipyard remained closed, and the U.S. Army had turned over most of its reservation for disposal but retained some property for the use of Army Reserves and the National Guard.

The city of Vancouver ushered in the new decade at midnight December 31, 1949, by annexing McLoughlin Heights area, with 14,000 residents. The federally-financed project had been home to shipyard workers during the war, and the number of Vancouver Housing Authority's tenants there was declining in 1950.

A few new industries opened in Clark County during the 1950s. The Alcoa plant continued producing aluminum, and the Crown-Zellerbach paper mill at Camas topped the important group of woods-based industries which had been so important to the area for many years.

In 1958, the last tenants moved out of the wartime McLoughlin Heights, where loss of temporary housing had impacted Vancouver population–down from 41,664 in 1950 to 32,464 in 1960. But a movement to the suburbs increased the total Clark County population—from 85,307 in 1950 to 93,809 in 1960.

Patrolmen Ted Slothower, left, and Robert Irwin manned three-wheeled motorcycles while checking Vancouver parking meters in 1955. Harry Wood, center, was traffic captain.

Port of Vancouver's Terminal 1, looking downstream from the Interstate 5 Bridge, 1956, with Columbia River Paper Company a short distance west.

St. Elmo Hotel was a prominent landmark, at the right, in this scene looking toward the new Interstate 5 freeway and the Columbia River in 1954.

The new four-lane freeway through Vancouver was ready for paving in January 1954, near Vancouver Barracks hospital (right).

Aerial shows Vancouver Barracks, lower left, also part of downtown at right and new Interstate 5 freeway in December 1954.

First vehicles rolled over new pavement after dedication of the freeway at Vancouver on March 31, 1955.

Toll gates were installed on the Interstate 5 Bridge late in 1959 so that money could be collected from motorists starting in 1960.

With nearly 700 employees, the SP&S was the largest industry at Vancouver in the late 1950s. Some worked on repairs, in the shop shown above.

Men applied black and silver paint to an SP&S steam locomotive, No. 539, prior to its move in September 1957 to Esther Short Park, where it would be the largest such engine on exhibit in the Pacific Northwest. It remained there for 40 years until it was moved to Battle Ground in 1997.

The efforts of several hundred volunteers, along with trucks and winches, were needed to move this old locomotive into place at Esther Short Park.

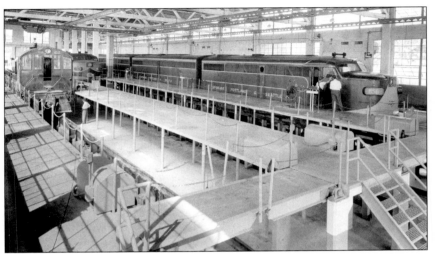

This 1955 photo shows the interior of the SP&S modern diesel-electric locomotive shops, built in 1948.

Wintry weather turned ponds into skating rinks in February 1958. These youngsters skated on Burnt Bridge Creek where it empties into Vancouver Lake.

The SP&S roundhouse, left center, could service 18 locomotives at one time with the aid of a turntable. This view is facing south, across an orchard and 39th Street.

A Spokane, Portland and Seattle Railway train arrived at Vancouver in 1951, at a time when the railroad company provided a major payroll in Clark County.

Dancers at Kiggins Bowl helped Vancouver celebrate its 1950 Cenaqua, the 125th anniversary of the establishment of Fort Vancouver.

The Grange, a long-time Clark County institution, was among numerous organizations participating in the Cenaqua celebration at Vancouver in 1950.

Main Street of Vancouver was the setting for parades and other events such as this march by a turkey and escorts.

Battle Ground celebrated a centennial in 1955 with costumed residents and a parade downtown.

The "Accordion Kids" of Blackburn Accordion School enlivened the Battle Ground centennial parade on July 29, 1955.

Vancouver's oldest industry in the 1950s was a brewery which produced Lucky Lager beer. The brewery had been established in the 1850s.

The Washougal branch of Pendleton Woolen Mills was second only to Crown Zellerbach paper mill in the Camas-Washougal area, for number of employees.

Archer-Daniels-Midland Company operated the huge grain elevator at the Port of Vancouver, shown here in the summer of 1955.

The Kaiser Foundation Hospital, above, closed in 1959 following the opening of Bess Kaiser Hospital in Portland, and was sold the same year to Columbia View Manor Corporation for use as a nursing home.

Vancouver Memorial Hospital, formerly Clark General Hospital at 3400 Main Street, dated back to 1929. Here it is seen from the air, in 1955.

Barnes Veterans Administration Hospital, successor to Barnes General Hospital, occupied wartime buildings south of Fourth Plain Boulevard.

Clark County Hospital at 2514 T Street can be seen at the center of this photo, and the VA Hospital at upper left.

In 1954, St. Joseph Hospital graduated its last nursing class.

These nurses were honored in 1955 for service at Clark County Hospital, located on Fourth Plain Boulevard near the Barnes VA Hospital. The county hospital was closed in late 1968.

St. Joseph Hospital, the county's only hospital for many years, cared for patients at 500 East 12th Street, Vancouver. The five-story brick hospital building, shown above, was opened in 1911.

Looking north in the 900 block of Main Street, about 1950.

Members of the Downtown Social Club, organized in the Ford Building in 1954, moved their activities later to 810 Washington Street.

Fort Vancouver Regional Library was pleased with this new bookmobile, ready for service in Clark and Skamania Counties in 1952. Among residents inspecting the vehicle at 1511 Main Street were, from the left, Clark County Commissioner T. C. McCamey, Vancouver Mayor Ralph Carter, Library Board Chairman Fred Mason, Eugene Rohrer and Irwin Zeller.

Passers-by could check the time on the clock near the Seattle First National Bank at 714 Main Street, pictured here in 1957.

Spic-N-Span at 1411 Washington Street advertised itself in the 1950s as "the streamlined drive-in." This is a drive-through burger restaurant, popular with teen cruisers in the 1950s and '60s.

Photo shows progress on new location of Interstate 5 freeway, north of Vancouver, in late 1958. The old route at the right would continue to carry local traffic through Hazel Dell.

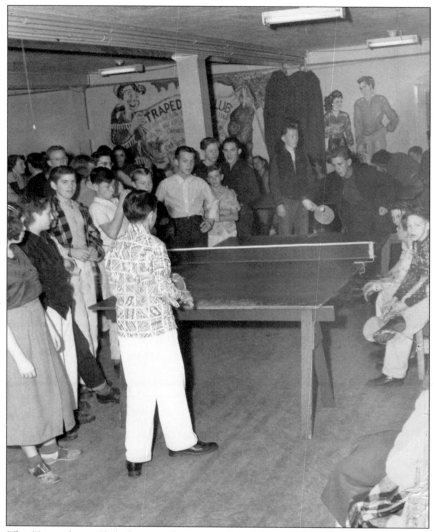

The Trapedero Club for youths opened at Memorial Hall, 13th Street and Broadway, in 1944 and continued active in the 1950s and early '60s. Its last home was at the Marshall Center.

Don Campbell turned the first shovelful of dirt in 1954 for construction of a new building at 8th and Grant streets. Campbell, business manager of *The Columbian* at the time, later headed the paper as co-publisher with his brother Jack.

Leroy Dolan, foreground, Viola Eaton and other linotype operators were vital employees in the "hot metal" process of producing *The Columbian*.

While waiting for completion of this new building, *The Columbian* employees continued publishing Vancouver's daily newspaper at 1000 Broadway.

The Columbian's advertising department was crowded before its move to new quarters in August 1955. Pat Crombie is the employee at the far right, and ad salesman Bob McCain is seated at front left.

Newspaper "back shops" before the days of offset publishing always required printers. Tom Harlan is *The Columbian* printer at right, in 1955.

This ritual team from Vancouver Elks Lodge won first place in state competition in 1956. The Elks played a prominent role in downtown Vancouver for many years.

National Guard troops served as an honor guard for Governor and Mrs. Albert Rosellini and Dr. Dwight Baird, new president of Clark College, at the dedication of the college's 60-acre campus in 1958.

Homecoming Queen Beverly Clawson (later Beverly Boydston) and Clark College President Paul Gaiser admired a college mascot statue installed in 1955. Bill Ware, student body president, is seated at the right.

Aerial view of Clark College in 1958, looking northeast.

Hudson's Bay High School students were eager for the opening of their new school in 1956.

After tours of the building on February 3, 1956, students were admitted for the first Hudson's Bay High School classes on February 6.

The names of most pioneer Clark County schools were abandoned when districts consolidated and buildings were closed. However, Glenwood's name survived in this new school, Glenwood Heights, built in 1956.

In February 1954, Evergreen School District razed the Mill Plain school, formerly the district's Union High School.

Some early-day schools had been converted into homes or stood empty in the 1950s. This is the old Highland Elementary School in northern Clark County.

Students pursued class work diligently at St. James Catholic School, 47th and Franklin streets, in 1956, the same year the school was dedicated. Youths mostly from Providence Academy attended the school, which was renamed Our Lady of Lourdes - St. James later.

At the Providence building in 1956, Sister Scholastica Mary tried out a spinning wheel formerly operated by Mother Joseph, first Superior of the Sisters of Charity of Providence at Vancouver.

Nuns of the Sisters of Charity of Providence enjoyed a card game in 1956 at Providence Academy, 400 East 10th Street (Evergreen Boulevard). Bridge and canasta were favorites for the nuns.

Despite sandbagging, part of East First Street was flooded under the Interstate 5 Bridge in 1956.

The Columbia River flooded much of the low-lying farm area between Vancouver and Ridgefield in the spring of 1956.

This kind of watery scene in 1956 reminded residents of the need for stronger dikes in Clark County.

Flood waters forced Mr. and Mrs. Alfred Lott, above, and many other Camas-Washougal residents to move out temporarily in 1956.

After widespread use in World War II, radar became a popular item for policeman such as E. M. Jarvis of Vancouver, to check speeding motorists.

Vancouver Fire Department modernized its equipment with these two pumping engines in 1957.

Brewery and municipal buildings dominated two blocks east of Esther Short Park in the 1950s. Main Street is at the upper right.

Columbia Machine Works (now Columbia Machine Inc.) was part of a new industrial area developed on former wartime housing property east of the Interstate 5 Bridge in the 1950s.

Women staffed a production line at Bemis Bag Company in this 1957 photo. The company was one of several new industries bolstering the post-war economy.

Stacked cans of Washington Canners Cooperative awaited shipment in 1957. The California Packing Corporation also employed many people in Vancouver food processing at this time.

In late 1959, Ideal Cement Company was nearing completion of six cement silos just upstream from the Interstate railway bridge.

The Tom E. Lewis family was the last to move out of the wartime Vancouver Housing Authority Project on McLoughlin Heights in 1948. After the housing was removed, many new homes were built.

Archaeologists were uncovering relics of old Fort Vancouver in the 1950s. Frank Hjort, superintendent of Fort Vancouver National Monument, left, and Jerry Wagers examined wood debris from the stockade area.

MacArthur School, lower left, at the intersection of MacArthur Boulevard and Blandford Drive, had accommodated families of World War II shipyard workers, and was still in use at the time of this 1955 photo. Another wartime facility, the McLoughlin Heights shopping center (upper right), was still serving neighborhood residents, although on a smaller scale than during the war. MacArthur school classes ended in 1958. McLoughlin Heights was the largest of several temporary, federally-financed housing projects in the Vancouver area.

The 1960s

The 1960s decade was especially notable for the Cuban missile crisis, the building of the Berlin Wall, and United States entry into the Vietnam war. Domestic dissent also was increasing in the United States.

Locally, one of the major efforts focused on the rebuilding of McLoughlin Heights, with private homes replacing the temporary wartime units.

Urban renewal also was a priority for the oldest part of Vancouver, and the city razed old homes and other buildings.

Vancouver's downtown still attracted considerable business, in the years before the completion of shopping centers. J.C. Penney Company, Vancouver Hadley's and the CC Store still were active, with a variety of smaller stores along Main Street.

For commuters using the Interstate Bridge, the big news of the decade was the removal of tolls in 1966. Toll gates had been installed not long after the completion of a second span of the bridge in the late 1950s.

In this post-war World War II era, when people had more leisure time, recreational facilities were getting more stress. Community leaders called attention to the Orchard Hills Golf Club, enlarged in the 1960s at Washougal, and the Kiggins Bowl stadium, which seated 8,000 persons in Vancouver.

The brick St. James Catholic Church is part of a varied Washington Street landscape that includes business buildings and even plentiful trees. This view is dated 1968.

Richard Nixon campaigned in Vancouver on September 13, 1960, with wife Pat. A crowd estimated at 6,000 cheered the Republican.

The U.S. Grant House, serving at the time as a museum, suffered damage in the Columbus Day storm of 1962. Winds also toppled numerous trees on Officers Row and elsewhere.

After riding through streets lined with flags, Richard Nixon (at bottom of photo) spoke from Clark County courthouse steps. He lost a close race for president to John Kennedy in November 1960.

Winds gusting up to 92 miles an hour blew down numerous trees in Esther Short Park on October 12, 1962.

A news story described Pearson Air Park "a massive junkyard" of overturned planes and twisted hangars after the 1962 Columbus Day windstorm. This is one of the planes.

Roofs, porches and other fixtures of homes also took a battering in the 1962 storm, the area's worst in decades.

A large plywood output helped the Pacific Northwest economy in the 1960s. Among the companies involved was International Paper Company, which operated a plywood plant and lumber mill at Chelatchie Prairie.

Logs still were plentiful when International Paper Company operated its Chelatchie Prairie mill. The photo above is dated 1964.

A Wagner Lumber Jack, with 35-ton capacity, handled logs at International Paper Company's barking and bucking center. This April 1961 photo shows Tum Tum Mountain a short distance away.

Plywood was stacked high at the Chelatchie mill, the leading industry in northern Clark County until it closed in 1979.

Workers manned about 400 sewing machines at Jantzen Knitting Mills in 1964. Jantzen finally closed the business in 1998 after about 50 years.

At the Jantzen Knitting Mills warehouse, women checked boxes of sportswear waiting for shipment. Jantzen was especially noted for its swim suits.

Production continued strong at the Alcoa (Aluminum Company of America) plant west of Vancouver in the years following World War II.

For many years the beer from Vancouver's brewery was known as Hop Gold but in later decades the workers produced Lucky Lager.

A Spokane, Portland and Seattle railway yardmaster at Vancouver talked to yard crews over an intercom, about 1961.

No. 16 paper machine helped boost Crown Zellerbach Corporation production at Camas in 1963.

Part of downtown Camas is visible at the lower right in this view of the Crown Zellerbach complex, in 1963. Railroad tracks cut through the center and upper left of the photo.

The weaving room at Pendleton Woolen Mills was running at capacity in 1969. This industry was Washougal's largest.

Carborundum Company operated on land purchased from the Port of Vancouver, near the Columbia River. In the 1960s the Port still was considering the possible development of a harbor at Vancouver Lake, not far from the Carborundum plant.

Long after most small mills had vanished from Clark County, the Bridge Shingle and Shake Company continued to be active on Route 3, Battle Ground. This is a 1965 photo.

A snowstorm shut down most Main Street business shortly before Christmas 1964. One of the best known stores at the time was Woolworth, at the far left of this photo, a fixture at 900 Main Street until 1976. The Penney's store later moved to the Vancouver Mall.

Clark County Fairgrounds provided ample facilities for the annual fair and other events in the 1960s. The fair started in 1868 at Vancouver, later was scheduled on Fourth Plain and at Battle Ground. William Wineberg donated 22 acres for the fair at the present site north of Vancouver, and the first fair there opened its gates in 1955.

Taverns flourished in 1964 near the Evergreen Hotel, which was in decline after 36 years as Vancouver's leading hotel.

Youths carried a dragon along Main Street in 1962 past Kessler's shoe store, operated at 907 Main Street by Max Kessler. Two other shoe stores and four clothing stores were among businesses active in the 800 and 900 blocks of Main Street.

Labor unions supported Mid-Columbia Manor, which dedicated the Smith Tower at 515 Washington Street in February 1965 as a retirement home for senior citizens.

Vancouver's old city hall at 712 Washington Street, in the foreground, was vacated in 1965 after construction of the present city hall. General Brewing Corporation was still operating the brewery just south of the old city hall at the time of this 1967 photo.

The paper mill payroll had been an important factor in the prosperity of Camas downtown, which is shown here in 1964. But merchants were facing increasing competition from shopping centers elsewhere in the area.

Starting in 1965, Camas began sprucing up its downtown with trees and shrubbery along NE Fourth Avenue. These two residents contributed their efforts in 1969.

One-Stop Shopping Center, which opened in 1947 partway between Camas and Washougal business districts, was reported to be one of the Northwest's first shopping centers.

Battle Ground gained favorable publicity for many years with the floats entered in the annual Portland Rose Festival parade. Hula girls waved from the town's 1960 entry. Vancouver also entered attractive floats in the floral parade.

One of Clark County's best known restaurants, the Totem Pole, drew customers at Hazel Dell's main intersection. This is a 1962 scene.

Television had cut into the movie theater business by the 1960s. One casualty of the changing times was the Liberty Theatre at Ridgefield.

Although Battle Ground's location is central in Clark County, the community's growth was slow for many years. Here is Main Street in 1964.

Work had started on a new freeway route through Hazel Dell at the time of this aerial, in June 1960, looking south. Old Pacific Highway is at the lower left and top center. The overpass at 78th Street for the new route is at the right center.

New housing and businesses clustered along or near the main routes north of Vancouver in the 1960s.

Mrs. John McAleer, left, U.S. Rep. Julia Butler Hansen and Mrs. Harold Burkitt, right, took part in a November 1, 1966, ribbon-snipping ceremony symbolizing the removal of tolls from the Interstate 5 Bridge.

Darrell Hedges of the Toll Bridge Authority accepted the final official toll on the Interstate 5 Bridge from Howard Burnham in 1966. Burnham's father, Allison Burnham, had been a leader in efforts to get a free bridge over the Columbia River.

Water traffic was brisk in the 1960s. One of the larger vessels passing along the Columbia River in 1969 was the barge Kenai, built to haul fertilizer.

Miss Vancouver contestants lined up for a photographer in 1960.

Young women competed at Vancouver, in earlier years, for the title of Miss Washington. Lauren Waddleton (Ms. Burien, center) won the coveted honor in 1964.

Kippy Lee Brinkman, Miss Everett (center), received congratulations from other contestants after winning the 1965 Miss Washington title.

Ben Padrow, a TV quiz show host, questioned a Fort Vancouver High School "High Q" team (top row) in a 1967 competition with West Linn, Oregon. The Vancouver team won.

In 1966, St. Joseph Hospital faced financial problems and there was talk of closure, but St. Joseph Community Hospital Association announced plans to construct a new facility.

Kathy Eaton, 1966 Clark County Fair queen, adjusted the cape of her successor, Nancy Arisman, in 1967. Both young women were students at Hudson's Bay High School, where Arisman (now Nancy Newlean) is presently a counselor.

Clark College cooperated with four citizen volunteers in building a telescope at the college in 1965 for a Goldendale observatory.

Vancouver Memorial Hospital completed a $3.2 million expansion and modernization project in 1965.

Helicopter pilot Richard Green lowered the top piece onto the new chime tower at Clark College in 1964. The Alumni Association financed the 66-foot structure.

St. Joseph Community Hospital took an option in 1967 on a site along Mill Plain Boulevard west of 92nd Avenue. In 1972, St. Joseph patients and staff moved to a new hospital at that location.

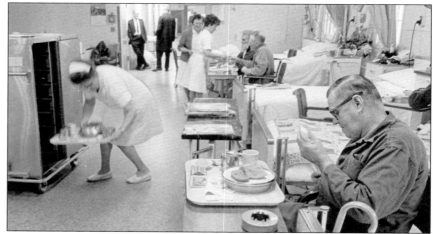

Veterans of two world wars and the Korean conflict were receiving care at Barnes Veterans Administration Hospital, at the time of this dinner scene, in December 1968.

Because of financial problems, the Clark County Commission closed Clark County Hospital at 2514 T Street, in late 1968.

Day Hilborn designed the Clark County Courthouse, which was completed in 1940. It was still adequate for the 1960s but demands for county services would rise rapidly as population increased in later years.

Former Vancouver Barracks property is the setting for the office building of Clark Public Utilities, which was known at the time of this 1966 photo as Clark County Public Utility District.

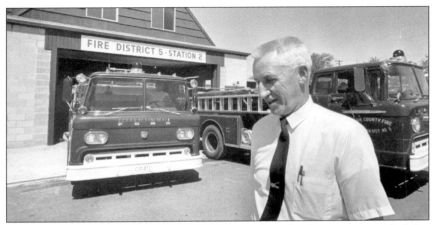

As more people moved into outlying areas, fire districts were needed for adequate protection. This fire station at 45th Street and St. Johns Road (in a 1969 photo) was just one of four stations serving District 5, where Francis Betzing was fire chief.

The federal government recognized the historical significance of Fort Vancouver by establishing a historical monument, which later was designated a historic site. The photo at left is dated 1962.

Providence Academy, in this 1969 aerial, is still an impressive landmark. In the 1870s the structure was described as the largest building north of San Francisco. The nuns operated a school, orphanage and hospital in Vancouver's earliest years.

Sisters Rita Maureen, left, and Jeanne Marie of the Sisters of Charity of Providence accepted a bronze plaque of a Vancouver pioneer, Mother Joseph, in 1968. The donor was St. Joseph Hospital medical staff, represented by Dr. Robert Bedrossian, second from left, and Dr. Samuel Osborn.

In early 1962, the National Park Service (NPS) resolved an access problem with Pearson Airpark, clearing the way for development at Fort Vancouver National Historic Site. At the time the NPS was displaying this emblem of the Hudson's Bay Company, which operated Fort Vancouver in fur-trading days, starting in 1825.

An urban renewal project cleared away numerous old homes and other buildings west of Esther Short Park and north of the Spokane, Portland and Seattle railway tracks in the early 1960s.

Before its move to Esther Short Park for use by the Old Slocum House Theatre Company, the Slocum House was used as a paper mill office.

The Old Slocum House, once owned by a prominent Vancouver merchant, appeared forlorn before it was moved to Esther Short Park to be used for amateur theatricals.

A victim of urban renewal, Mill Way Café at 600 West Fifth Street had catered to hungry residents in earlier years. This is a 1962 photo.

Employees of *The Columbian* checked first newspapers coming off the press after conversion to offset printing in 1968. Jack Campbell, co-publisher, is at the far right, alongside Maurice (Morrie) Shore, production manager. Co-publisher, Don Campbell is walking towards camera near the center of the photo.

NAAR VANCOUVER CENTRUM

ΕΔΩΘΕ ΔΙΑ ΤΟ ΒΑΝΚΟΥΒΕΡ

STADEN'S CENTER

NEDE BYEN

STADTMITTE

TIL BYEN

はんえい街

시내중심가

由此路上市场去

A sign in several languages pointed the way to town in 1963, for foreign seamen taking some brief time off from ships docked at the Port of Vancouver.

Ernest Endicott carved this Plainsman, a symbol of Evergreen High School, for presentation to the school by the graduating class of 1968.

Pacific Inland Navigation Company leased the old Stebco mill site in 1961 at 6305 Lower River Road and consolidated its operations there. The company, organized in 1937 to operate barges and towboats, had moved an office to Vancouver in 1941. By the 1960s the company was active along the coast, in addition to the Columbia and Snake rivers.

The 1970s

For headline-grabbing attention, a tornado and rock festival rated near the top during the 1970s in Clark County.

In that era, parents were dismayed by the new counterculture, which was epitomized in their minds by hippies, drugs and rock music. Thousands of footloose young people startled residents in 1970 by converging on a Washougal farm for the Sky River Rock Festival, lasting about a week.

A tornado, rare for Clark County, killed six persons and caused extensive damage in 1972 near Fourth Plain Boulevard and Andresen Road. Peter S. Ogden Elementary School was among buildings shattered.

On the commercial front, new shopping centers were starting to compete with the downtown. Tower Mall and Vancouver Mall both opened in the 1970s, the latter with 90 specialty shops and stores.

Western Electric Company closed in 1975 but the outlook for more high-tech jobs seemed bright, especially after Tektronix, Inc., and Hewlett-Packard announced plans to build plants.

In the criminal category, residents were fascinated by the hijacker D.B. Cooper who parachuted out of an airplane with $200,000 in 1971 over northern Clark County or the area nearby. Law enforcement officers never located him.

Columbia River High School band, with Adair Hilligoss in charge, paraded in 1977.

Clark County residents were shocked when thousands of youths began arriving at a farm north of Washougal in the last week of August 1970 for the Sky River rock festival. Customers above perused wares along the camp's main thoroughfare.

Some concession stands at the rock festival advertised drugs. This and other festivals of the era put strong emphasis on rock music.

Chief Criminal Deputy Sheriff Gene Cotton explained an injunction to a rock festival denizen named Puzzleman. But a heedless crowd continued to swarm to the property, and soon was estimated at 20,000.

Some long-haired arrivals at Sky River had gathered around a small fire and others prepared a makeshift meal.

A participant in the rock festival labeled this debris "American Dream Memorial," which fitted the mood of protests and revolt against authority prevalent at the time.

The "Freedom Tree" at Orchards, tied with a yellow ribbon, expressed the hopes of Clark County residents who wanted captured troops returned, about 1973. Sponsors were Evergreen Jaycees and Washingtonians for the Return of Servicemen from Vietnam.

Tractors hauled out rubble and debris from Peter S. Ogden Elementary School following a tornado on April 5, 1972.

Rescuers carried out one of the victims of the tornado that killed six persons and injured about 300 at Vancouver. Five persons died at the Waremart discount store.

Heavy equipment was used at the Waremart store to clear wreckage. The April 5, 1972, tornado was centered at Andresen Road and Fourth Plain Boulevard.

Pieces of the Waremart roof were strewn over the landscape after the deadly wind, a rare occurrence for Clark County.

The six Vancouver tornado victims are commemorated by a marker at Evergreen Memorial Gardens, installed in 1973.

Emergency workers were swamped by injured people following the Vancouver tornado, which also caused an estimated $3 million damage.

Western Electric Company started at Vancouver with a small work force including this woman.

B. W. Northrup, general manager of the planned Western Electric Company plant at Vancouver, displayed an intricate piece of company equipment in 1970. Arrival of the industry was major news.

Tektronix, a company based in Beaverton, Oregon, moved a branch plant to Vancouver in 1978. This is an interior view of activity in the building where Western Electric had closed in 1975.

A helicopter brought in a heater-ventilator unit for Western Electric Company's plant. This was January 1971 and the employees had started moving into a new building on Lewis and Clark Highway. By late summer the company had more than 800 employees.

Workers maneuvered a 3,000-pound device onto a platform at International Paper Company's mill at Chelatchie Prairie in 1976. A helicopter then lifted the equipment to the top of a nearby building for installation, as required by state pollution control officials.

Tiny but powerful Tektronix devices such as these "may revolutionize Clark County's future," *The Columbian* predicted. High-tech industries were bringing in new payrolls.

Sylvia Stephens, one of the early Tektronix employees at Vancouver, worked on a cable assembly.

A production line turned out milk cartons in 1975 at the Weyerhaeuser Carton Division, on West 31st Street, Vancouver.

Boise Cascade paper plant, shown here in 1974, had succeeded Columbia River Paper Company about 1963. The earlier business was established in 1923 at the site of the old Pittock-Leadbetter mill. Production of lumber along the waterfront at and near this location dated back to about 1890.

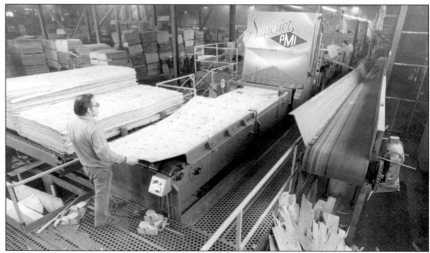

This is a 1979 production line scene at Fort Vancouver Plywood, which had started as a privately-owned company at the Port of Vancouver in the 1920s, occupying former shipyard facilities.

Fort Vancouver Plywood Company continued active as an employee-owned cooperative in the 1970s.

Cans rolled down to waiting employees at the Northwest Packing Company, a Port of Vancouver tenant, in 1978.

Using jackhammers, Carborundum Company employees broke up silicon carbide produced by heating large amounts of coke and sand, in 1970.

Crown Zellerbach Corporation continued improvements at its Camas mill, later acquired by James River Corporation. This photo is dated 1975.

Port of Vancouver trades extensively with Asia and other parts of the world. In 1976, longshoremen were loading housing units for Arabia.

Occasional strikes shut down work at the Port of Vancouver and other West Coast ports in earlier years. These pickets patrolled a Vancouver dock in January 1972.

Small boats have found a moorage at the Port of Camas-Washougal. Hank Sadewasser, a Washougal pioneer, visited there in 1979.

A big trend toward mechanization was improving the efficiency of the work force at the Port of Vancouver. The vehicle above had no trouble handling large beams in 1977.

The Ampere building and Ross substation (in rear) preceded the Dittmer Control Center at Bonneville Power Administration's Ross complex in Hazel Dell. BPA employs more than 900 persons at the Ross complex in 2000.

Bonneville Power Administration, named for an early western explorer, opened the Dittmer Control Center at Hazel Dell in 1971. The system console could control the entire BPA high-voltage grid.

High voltage test equipment provided a science-fiction atmosphere to the Ampere building, operated by the Bonneville Power Administration at Hazel Dell, east of old Highway 99.

A wrecker's ball battered the former St. Joseph Hospital in 1974.

A possible merger of St. Joseph Community Hospital (above) and Vancouver Memorial Hospital was a lively topic in 1977, when this photo was taken. St. Joseph's name was later changed to Southwest Washington Hospital, and finally Southwest Washington Medical Center.

A declining patient load resulted in the elimination of numerous beds in 1978 and 1979 at Vancouver Memorial Hospital. Southwest Washington Hospital, which owned Vancouver Memorial as well as St. Joseph Hospital, was working on merger plans for the hospitals.

Robert Hidden and his sons bought the Providence Academy building in 1969 and converted it into an area for offices and shops. He received an award 10 years later from the Washington Trust for Historic Preservation for his efforts at historic preservation.

Plans to tear down the old Fort Vancouver High School south of Fourth Plain Boulevard and west of Main stirred much controversy starting in 1970.

The old high school included a big auditorium that many residents believed should be preserved and used. Harley Mays, Robert Hidden and others joined a committee to save the school as a multi-use community center.

Despite efforts of opponents such as those gathered above, Vancouver Housing Authority tore down the old Fort Vancouver High School to make way for housing. Demolition was completed in early 1973.

New area schools featured modern facilities, such as this media center at Columbia River High School, which opened in 1969 at Hazel Dell. The photo dates from 1977.

The protest trend of the 1960s and '70s had spread to some schools. This 1976 teacher picket line was set up in Evergreen School District.

Increasing numbers of youths sought a two-year education at Clark College, which had enrollment of 3,500 full-time-equivalent students in 1976.

Vancouver was proud of its new City Hall, shown here in 1973, and the adjoining new police station.

Mayor Jim Justin, center, was among officials donning T-shirts in 1979 to promote the city. Others, from left, are City Council members Ross Hollister, Bryce Seidl, Martin Wolf, Ethel Lehmann, and Rose Besserman.

First Federal Savings and Loan Association, later known as Community First Federal Savings, occupied a new brick building at 12th and Main streets. This is now the main office of the First Independent Bank.

Looking north from Fifth Street at Main in 1976, downtown Vancouver.

Main Street seemed lively in 1976, looking south from the 900 block.

A guitarist entertained customers at Corners of the Mouth Coffeehouse, 106 West Sixth Street, in 1975.

The Smith Tower was a vantage point for this view of Vancouver downtown in December 1970. Washington Street is at the left.

Dancers found ample room to show off their skills, downtown in 1978. The Arts building stands out against the skyline.

In 1979, St. James Catholic Church celebrated the 95th anniversary of the building, which had been the cathedral (headquarters) of the Diocese of Nesqually, in 1884 when the cornerstone was laid. Catholic history at Vancouver dates back to 1838.

Vancouver firefighters used a training tower south of Mill Plain Boulevard on Grace Street at the time of this photo in 1976. Vancouver city shops were situated at the upper left.

Women volunteers Marjorie Yinger, Susan Nelson and Michele Larson of Clark County Fire District 11 in the Battle Ground area demonstrated their firefighting abilities in 1975.

First aid was an increasing responsibility of Clark County's fire departments in the 1970s. This vehicle in Fire District 6 at Hazel Dell provided needed equipment.

Vancouver Fire Chief Steve Groesbeck handed out fire prevention material to youngsters in 1972, with encouragement from Smokey Bear (Mrs. Mel Tandberg).

Girls of the Spartans Drum and Bugle Corps, co-sponsored by the Salmon Creek American Legion post, practiced in 1977.

A rifle squad fired a salute at a 1976 Veterans Day ceremony in Camas, sponsored by the American Legion and Veterans of Foreign Wars.

Clarence the Clown and his Girl Troop displayed their agility at the 1977 Amboy Territorial Days.

Ridgefield royalty promoted the town's July 4th celebration in 1975. Left to right they are: front row, Denise Kolshinski, Theresa Thomasson, Darci Hyatt, Melissa Ladgerwood and Lisa Schurman; middle row, Shirley Johns, Karen Andre, Janie Zumstein; back row, Carol Kraus, Desiree Brookshire, Kim Budde.

Cascade Park was in its infancy at the time of this aerial view, in 1971.

Traffic was relatively light on Fourth Plain Boulevard through Orchards in 1970, as compared with later years. The largest building pictured here was Danielson's Thriftway, adjacent to the First Independent Bank.

Orchards Feed Mill retained the atmosphere of a past agricultural era. Rowland Goff had worked there 27 years when he was photographed in 1979.

Construction of Vancouver Mall, shown here in 1976, would bring big changes in shopping habits of Clark County residents.

Faye and Lenual Wedding chatted with a customer, right, at Yacolt Mercantile in 1978.

Downtown Ridgefield, three miles from the freeway, did not seem to miss the lack of traffic. Jaywalking was no problem, as indicated here in 1973.

La Center advertised its centennial in 1974. The Old Pacific Highway carried traffic through town and past the old hotel, shown in the background.

Eager crowds rolled out carts for the opening of the Valu-Mart Discount Department Store at the Tower Mall shopping center (now the Town Plaza) in May 1971.

Vancouver Mayor Lloyd Stromgren, left, Nancy Peterson, Miss Washington 1970, and Douglas Weisfeld, vice-president of Weisfeld's Incorporated, were among notables turning out for the Valu-Mart opening.

Another key tenant, Safeway, opened June 2, 1971, at Tower Mall, on Mill Plain Boulevard near Devine Road, along with a card shop and the nearby Pizza Haven.

Commuters complained about traffic jams and long delays on Interstate 5 freeway near the Interstate Bridge. Here, vehicles are backed up along Washington Street.

A freight train rolled along the railroad tracks, crossing two streets and two sections of Interstate 5 freeway in this 1976 view, with the Interstate Bridge in the foreground and Vancouver's downtown at the upper center.

Grading for Interstate 205, above, was under way in 1973 although the Interstate 205 Bridge would not be completed until nearly a decade later.

Blue Star Highway was just another name for the Pacific Highway, part of which is now known as Highway 99.

The former Kaiser shipyard near Highway 14 still offered some industrial potential in the 1970s. The area took on a new name, Gilmore Industrial Center, about 1970. In World War II, the shipyard employment had peaked at more than 38,000.

Since shortly after World War II Army Reserve troops had trained at Vancouver Barracks. The marchers above were photographed in 1971.

Small planes flew in and out Pearson Airpark, a former Army Air Corps train-ing field near east Fifth Street taken over by the city after World War II. Kenneth Puttkamer managed the field in the 1970s.

For about a decade starting in 1966, the National Park Service was active in reconstructing Fort Vancouver. This photo shows 1973 work.

Volunteers have manned a railroad exhibit set up in the Clark County Historical Museum basement. Forrest Baker awaited visitors there in 1976.

The 1980s

Economic problems troubled the Vancouver area early in the 1980s, highlighted in 1982 by the closing of the Carborundum Company plant and Del Monte cannery. Two of the best-known industries, Alcoa and General Brewing Company, closed later in the decade, although a new company, Vanalco, reopened the aluminum plant in 1987.

The name of the biggest business, Crown-Zellerbach Corporation, was dropped when James River Corporation took over at the Camas paper mill in 1986.

To aid the area's economy, local leaders organized the Columbia River Economic Development Council in 1982.

The opening of the $175-million Interstate 205 bridge between Vancouver and Portland in 1982 was a major factor foreshadowing new growth. The span provided new access into the area east of Vancouver, where Genstar Development Company had acquired much property from MacKay and MacDonald.

But a news event outside Clark County created the biggest sensation inside the County—the eruption of Mount St. Helens. Residents could view the huge plume of ash from the shattered peak in 1980, and some ash was scattered in the county, although most drifted eastward a long distance.

A barge-mounted crane lifted a collapsed crane that had plunged into the Columbia River at the Interstate 205 Bridge. The fallen crane had toppled from the structure at the left, killing two workers.

This is another view of the Interstate 205 bridge supports that were in place by 1980, seven miles east of downtown Vancouver.

Workmen inspected crumpled wreckage of the accident that killed two men at the partially completed Interstate 205 Bridge on December 3, 1980.

Residents knew the Interstate 205 freeway project was near completion when pavement was rolled out in 1982.

The Interstate 205 Glenn Jackson Bridge was a catalyst in the development in Cascade Park and east Clark County in the 1980s and '90s. This view is looking east, with Government Island and the Oregon bank of the Columbia River at the right.

The Interstate 5 Bridge continued to carry tens of thousands of vehicles daily between Vancouver and Portland in the 1980s. Heavy usage required occasional traffic-disrupting repairs. First traffic had rolled over the old bridge in 1917.

Michelle Chapell displayed a sign in 1985 warning of possible problems on the Interstate 5 Bridge, where trucks are numerous.

Shoppers swarmed through Vancouver Mall on a Friday, the day after Thanksgiving 1983.

An impressive entrance lured customers to the west side of Vancouver Mall, where Meier and Frank operates a department store. One of the other major mall tenants, JC Penney Company, had moved from downtown Vancouver.

Boise Cascade Corporation remained a major employer at Vancouver. Rocky Stevens explained the paper production machinery to Covington Junior High School students in 1987.

Newly-installed pollution control equipment cost the Carborundum Company $10 million.

Good logs were harder to find in the 1980s for Pacific Northwest mills, such as Fort Vancouver Plywood.

Lee Ann Moore operated a large Pendleton Woolen Mill machine as a weaver at Washougal in 1980.

The federal government opened a Nursing Skilled Care unit at the Veterans Administration Hospital in 1985.

James River Corporation acquired the Crown Zellerbach mill at Camas in 1986. This is a 1988 view looking south toward the Columbia River and Lady Island (upper right).

Hewlett-Packard Company started operations at a temporary plant near Fort Vancouver High School in 1979, but soon moved further east. The above building, in a 1988 photo, is at Southeast 164th Avenue and 34th Street.

Personnel manager Dennis Chapman led Kyocera high-tech employees in a morning exercise after company announcements.

An increasing population had bolstered church congregations in the suburbs. Here, Reverend Bill Ritchie speaks in 1986 at Crossroads Community Church, one of Clark County's largest churches.

The atrium in the Tektronix building at 164th Avenue and Mill Plain Boulevard was sometimes used for quick meetings.

Workmen imbedded the logo of SEH America in concrete during 1983 construction. By the end of the 1990s decade the company had more than 1,600 employees, second largest of any Clark County industry.

Blind and deaf students have received specialized training at long-time Vancouver schools. The State School for the Deaf, at the first site of old Fort Vancouver, is shown in a 1981 photo.

Alan Aldridge directed the 1982 band at Prairie High School, which had opened three years earlier in Battle Ground School District.

One of the oldest schools in the Vancouver area is Salmon Creek Elementary. Salmon Creek teacher Nancy Woodbury read in 1988 from a Mother Joseph book that she had written and her class had helped illustrate.

Fort Vancouver High School girls volleyball team celebrated a 1985 victory at Evergreen High School.

Enthusiastic youngsters pursued a pig at the Amboy Territorial Days celebration in 1986.

Lance Benson, right, of Gaiser Junior High School, plunged to first place during a 1985 district junior high school track meet at Evergreen High School.

Sanjai Sharpe of Vancouver performed a Thai classical dance at the 1984 International Festival in Esther Short Park.

Each summer brings community celebrations in Clark County. One of these, the 1980 Hazel Dell Parade of Bands, attracted the spectators shown above.

A Bavarian dancer received instructions from Eula Slack of the Aloha Kaanohi Revue at Vancouver's 1986 Sausage Festival, sponsored by St. Joseph's Catholic Church.

Food booths attracted hungry residents at the 1987 Clark County Fair, a long-time fixture north of Vancouver.

The Port of Vancouver had sponsored a major rehabilitation of Vancouver Lake west of Vancouver in the 1980s, after earlier plans for a commercial harbor that had failed to materialize. Wind surfers and others are pictured at the lake in 1984.

Mt. Hood is visible in the distance in this 1985 recreational scene at Vancouver Lake.

Odette Millner and Robert Arbogast of the Nutcracker ballet spoke to a Columbia Arts Center audience after a 1987 performance.

The Broadway Theatre at Broadway and Evergreen Boulevard offered an alternative to TV before it was torn down in 1982.

The City of Vancouver supported the conversion of a former church building into the Columbia Arts Center at 400 West Evergreen Boulevard.

Becky Reinhart polished a Broadway Theatre counter top while Michelle Weeks dipped up popcorn in 1984.

Vancouver boosters have added some artistic touches to make the downtown more attractive. These are arches at the south end of Main Street, photographed in 1985.

Shrubs and flowers have helped beautify Main Street, and are protected by concrete barriers. A couple hustled past this island of vegetation near Seventh Street in 1981.

Sculptor Pat Ryan of Oswego, Oregon and Janet Moulton chatted in 1987 beside a sundial at "Secretaries' Island," 11th and Main Street, Vancouver.

Maureen Higgins, a puppeteer, maneuvered a character in a Tears of Joy Theatre production in 1989. The Vancouver-based company has staged many shows in recent years.

Colorful murals of area history decorated the walls of the Clark County branch of Seattle First National Bank at 1103 Main Street. The firm also operated a Vancouver branch at 714 Main Street.

Crowds jammed the CC Store, a long-time Vancouver business at 715 Main Street, for a final sale in June 1981. William L. Garrison operated the store.

Sol Myerson and his wife Frances closed their self-service shoe store at 819 Main Street in 1981. The business dated from the late 1920s.

The two local branches of Seattle First National Bank were combined in the downtown's biggest building, Seafirst Financial Center, which opened in 1983.

Bill Ward waited for business behind the bar in Alexander's Restaurant and Lounge at the old Evergreen Hotel in 1980. The five-story building located at Fifth and Main Street in Vancouver is now an Evergreen Retirement Inn. The former restaurant is now a dining room.

City of Vancouver decided in 1981 to buy Pete Piazza's Vancouver Bowl at 8th and C streets and demolish it, to make way for a future arts and conference center. This is a 1981 interior shot at the long-time landmark.

Firefighters battled a 1985 blaze at the Bank Tavern, 106 West Sixth Street, where the North Bank Tavern is now located.

Men from the carpenter's apprentice and training program installed a roof on the new gate house at Officers Row in 1988.

Visitors simulated the fur trading era in a 1980 camp set up outside the Fort Vancouver stockade.

A 1989 carriage ride provided a pleasant diversion near the parade ground bandstand on Officers Row.

Portland school children frolicked on a 1985 visit to the interior of the restored Fort Vancouver stockade.

A museum featuring aviation history has been developed at Pearson Airpark, where visitors examined a British fighter plane in 1988.

Lee Hanson cleaned a sculpture at Esther Short Park in 1985. Afterward it was sprayed with a wood preservative.

In 1989, Vince Ast was restoring a hand pump which had provided Washougal with water in pioneer times.

Commercial signs competed for attention at Hazel Dell, in the major business district north of Vancouver.

Old Highway 99 is turned into a festival area for the annual Hazel Dell Parade of Bands. The above activity took place in 1982.

A variety store and drug store still were among businesses operating in downtown Camas in 1983.

Most La Center businesses clustered along one block, and there was still a rural atmosphere in the surrounding countryside at the time of this 1983 photo.

Barbara Waggener, above, and other residents promoted the development of the museum at an old Amboy church building.

Passengers boarded a Chelatchie Prairie Railroad train for a 1982 excursion. In early years, the railroad had hauled logs and other freight as well as passengers.

The 1990s

Clark County records for home and apartment construction and the opening of new businesses were toppled during the 1990s.

Population figures also told some of the growth story: up from 238,053 in 1990 to 337,000 in 1999, a gain of nearly 100,000 in the county; and from 46,380 to 135,100 for Vancouver in the same period. The city's population growth, helped along by annexations, placed it solidly in fourth place among Washington state municipalities.

The Tektronix plant closed in 1990, eliminating 1,300 jobs. But the high-tech industries generally had been thriving in the 1990s, and continued to play an important role of providing jobs for thousands of county residents in the century's final decade.

The city of Vancouver was pushing ahead with plans for downtown revitalization, in and near Esther Short Park, and the Heritage condominiums were nearing completion early in 2000 on two blocks north of the park.

The waterfront east of Interstate 5 Bridge was in transition in the 1990s, with completion of housing units, some commercial development and other activity. Further downstream, the Port of Vancouver was preparing long-range plans for the development of 800 acres of land formerly owned by Alcoa.

Esther Short Park dominates much of this view, with First Interstate Tower (now Riverview Tower) at the upper left and Bank of America building at the upper right, circa 1998.

Long hallways at Vancouver Mall (later renamed Westfield Shoppingtown Vancouver) attracted residents who enjoy walking for exercise. These three, from left, Jo Golden, Elsie Sprague, and Barbara Barnes, walked three times a week in 1990, before the mall opened for business.

Musicians entertained a 1993 crowd at Vancouver Mall, where a second-floor food court was a popular new feature.

In the 1990s the Farmers' Market lured many Clark County people to Vancouver's downtown.

The Kiggins is the lone survivor among movie theaters that flourished on Main Street in earlier years.

Construction started in 1993 on Underwriters Laboratories overlooking LaCamas Lake at Camas.

From the top of the First Interstate Tower, now called Riverview Tower, the site of the proposed Heritage Place condominiums, is visible at the right in this photo. The Columbia River is in the background of this late 1990s picture.

New industries continued to open in Clark County in the 1980s and '90s. Camas City Adminstrator Lloyd Halverson is pictured at the Sharp Electronic site in 1990.

Two ships waited offshore in the Columbia River near the Port of Vancouver. A portion of Hayden Island occupies the right foreground in this view, looking toward the eastern neighborhoods of Vancouver, and Mount Hood.

Officers checked underbrush near Blandford Drive in October 1997 for a suspected bank robber, who was later captured near Fort Vancouver High School.

Ready for action, Vancouver Police Department's special response team moved out in October 1997 to hunt for a robbery suspect who had escaped after a shootout. Officers shot and killed two other suspects.

At the end of the 1990s, Clark County residents were discussing possible future use of Camp Bonneville near Camas. The United States Army had declared the property surplus to its needs.

Area law enforcement officers and their dogs stood at attention during a 1990 Clark County Courthouse ceremony in which a sheriff's office dog, Lucky, was honored with the sheriff's Award of Valor. A robbery suspect had shot and killed the dog during a chase.

Cheerleaders help create enthusiasm in Clark County schools. Here, Ridgefield cheerleaders were practicing a 1990 routine.

The Columbia River girls volleyball team, state champions, celebrated following a 1991 school assembly in the team's honor.

Looking southwest in 1991 on Clark College campus, from near the Chime Tower. The college occupies former Vancouver Barracks property.

Wal-Mart picked a key location, on Mill Plain Boulevard just west of Interstate 205, to construct a new store. Employees cheered at the store's opening in October 1998.

Brian Haberman had a smile for customers in 1991 at John's Shoes and Clothing, one of Battle Ground's oldest businesses.

The Market Place at Vancouver features restaurants and other small businesses. Sheryl Erz, right, showed off some items there from her Mercantile Collection in 1990.

Numerous older businesses continued to thrive among hundreds of new commercial ventures. Missy and Ben Goodwin, shown here, operated the Thrifty Feed Store on St. John's Road in 1992; it opened about 1948.

Clark County residents interested in historic preservation are especially proud of the Cedar Creek grist mill, situated near the Lewis River. Supporters have rehabilitated the mill, where farmers had brought grain starting in the 1870s.

School for the Deaf students travel to their homes elsewhere in the state on Friday. Misty Pupo, of Pasco, facing the camera, shared a good-bye hug with Elly Redford in 1991.

Teacher Pat Jones helped students prepare a Thanksgiving turkey at Vancouver's Pan Terra alternative school in 1991.

Computers are now basic equipment in Clark County schools. Drafting students Duane Nagel, Joe Calderone, and Scott Shoemaker, in front from left to right, worked on a 1990 project at Washougal High School.

In 1990, a teen-parent class at Columbia River High School provided student mothers an opportunity to attend classes and a chance for other students to work with children.

In 1990, Clark College completed the new Hawkins Hall in honor of deceased instructor Richard Hawkins. This photo shows the entry to the new hall and Foster and Hanna halls near Fort Vancouver Way.

Formerly Vancouver's first middle school, this ornate building at 3101 Main Street is now Vancouver School of Arts and Academics, a magnet school since 1996 for Vancouver youngsters of the 6th through 12th grades.

The Al Angelo Company broke ground in early 1999 on Heritage Place condominiums, a major downtown development on two city blocks at the bottom center of this picture. They are just north of Esther Short Park.

Padden Parkway, under construction in 1999 north of 78th Street, is expected to be completed in 2003 and will ease traffic congestion for east-west travel in Clark County. The route is planned to merge with 83rd Street where that street crosses over Interstate 205, in the center of this 1998 view looking east.

Here is a 1999 view of Padden Parkway, a new route formerly known as Padden Expressway.

The Jesus Northwest event packed the bleachers and the adjoining terrain at the Clark County fairgrounds in 1992.

A carnival midway, nationally known entertainers and many varied exhibits lured thousands of residents to the annual Clark County Fair in 1990s.

Vancouver mechanic Harvey Grice welcomed visitors to his stand during Vancouver's 1998 Chili Cookoff.

Aaron Lutz, left, Lance Gange and Megan Lutz maneuvered their water-filled bathtub in 1996 Camas Days competition.

A camera time exposure blended colors together as the rides spun around and moved up and down at the 1999 Clark County Fair.

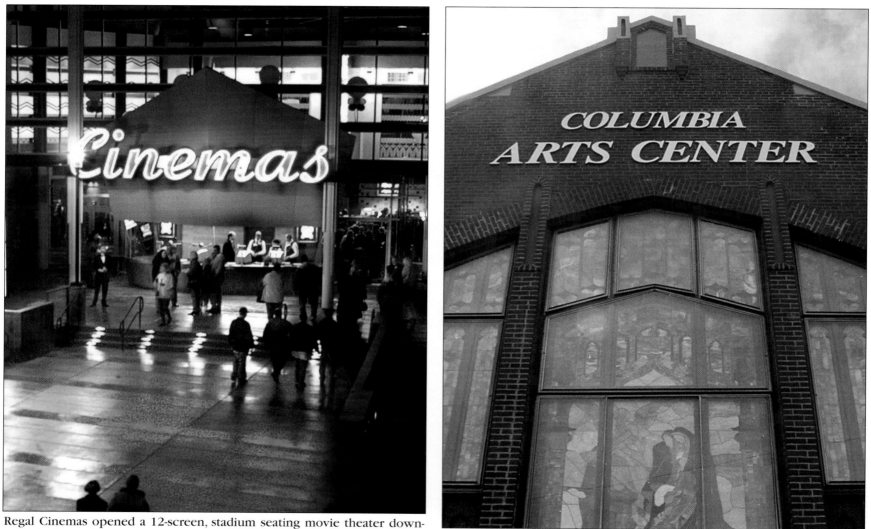

Regal Cinemas opened a 12-screen, stadium seating movie theater down-town in December 1998. Multiple-screen theaters had been built in other parts of the community in the past few years. The largest of all, Cascade Cinema, with 16 screens, opened in 1998 on SE 164th Avenue.

A long experiment using a former church building on West Evergreen Boulevard as an arts center ended in 1999. The City of Vancouver placed the property for sale in 2000 for commercial purposes.

Summer is time for fun at parks. A crowd relaxed while listening to jazz by Tom Grant at Vancouver's waterfront park in 1991.

A grimacing cowboy neared the end of his bull ride at the 1998 Clark County Fair. Varied attractions have helped keep attendance high at the annual fair north of Salmon Creek.

Nearly 1,500 students turned out for the opening of Evergreen School District's newest high school, Heritage, in September 1999.

The $21-million Heathman Lodge, with Hudson's Bar and Grill, was the highest-priced lodging facility in Clark County when it opened in late 1997 at 7801 N. E. Greenwood Drive, west of Westfield Shoppingtown Vancouver, formerly Vancouver Mall. Heathman Management Group of Portland built the lodge, featured by massive logs and inlaid stone floors.

Clark Public Utilities generating plant built by Cogentrix Energy, Inc., at 5201 NW Lower River Road produced its first power in 1997.

SEH America, Inc., a subsidiary of Shin-Etsu Company of Japan, manufactures silicon wafers. The plant at 4111 NE 112th Avenue employed more than 1,600 persons in 1999, second only to Hewlett-Packard among Clark County industries.

WaferTech, producing integrated circuits at Camas, was Clark County's fourth largest industry in 1999, with 850 employees.

The downtown Elks building, owned by Biggs Insurance Services at 105 West Evergreen Boulevard, has been listed on the National Register of Historic Places since 1989.

Vancouver/Clark Recreation Department opened the Frenchman's Bar regional park on the Columbia River five miles west of downtown Vancouver in 1997.

In the 1980s and '90s, new development in Cascade Park helped boost population in Clark County. The area is now annexed to Vancouver, bolstering the city's position as the fourth largest in Washington state.

Many new residential units now occupy waterfront property east of the Interstate 5 Bridge. This 1997 scene shows an area where the sidewalk had been rebuilt and widened and the bank reinforced, following the Columbia River flooding the previous year.

Unexpectedly strong winds startled Clark County residents on December 12, 1995. These office workers huddled for protection near the Seafirst Bank building in downtown Vancouver.

Nature's vagaries continue to make news locally and in other parts of the country. Here, an overflow of water slowed down a bicyclist on Columbia Way beneath the Interstate 5 Bridge in June 1997.

An arch at Fifth Street, near the former center of downtown, is a Vancouver landmark. The Farmers' Market sold its produce and other items at nearby stalls in the 1990s.

Flooding near the Vanalco plant and elsewhere in Clark County lowlands, in February 1996, reminded residents of the continuing power of the Columbia River, and previous major floods such as in 1894 and 1948. Salmon Creek contributed to the 1996 flooding. In the picture above, the waters have cut a driveway near Northeast Salmon Creek Avenue and 136th Street.

Lewis River on the border of Clark and Cowlitz Counties rampaged in February 1996, flooding much of Woodland. President Bill Clinton visited the community shortly after the disaster. Woodland lies mostly in Cowlitz County but with a small area inside Clark County.

Stu Degan-Smith helped clean up at Columbia Business Park, in December 1995, after a windstorm devastated a boat moorage. The business park occupies the site of the World War II Kaiser Shipyard.

As Tim Hall looked on, manager Ray Hill checked damage to the San Juan Apartments at 10400 NE Stutz Road, resulting from a windstorm in December 1995. Hill managed the apartments.

Washington State University Vancouver opened its new Salmon Creek campus in June 1996. This is one of three such WSU branches in the state. The building pictured right, houses Student Services.

Strikes by longshoremen occasionally shut down shipping in the earlier years, but for a long time business has been steady and peaceful along Vancouver's waterfront. The vessels above were photographed near of the railroad bridge in 1998.

Night lights were reflected from the campus of Washington State University, Vancouver.

Fort James Corporation succeeded James River Corporation in 1997 as the operator of the Camas paper mill pictured here. The plant, employing 1,500 workers in 1999, was the leading Clark County industry for many earlier years in number of employees. H.L. Pittock a Portland, Oregon, newspaper publisher, was instrumental in establishing the mill and the adjoining town, known originally as LaCamas.

In 1994 the City of Vancouver installed this statue of Ilchee, daughter of a noted Columbia River Indian chief, on the Waterfront Renaissance trail at 1701 SE Columbia River Drive.

Sculptor R.W. (Bill) Bane completed this sculpture in 1996. The statue of Carlton Bond, former commanding officer of the U.S. Army Air Corp's Pearson Field, stands in front of the Pearson Air Museum on East Fifth Street.

Officers Row, acquired by the City of Vancouver in 1984 from the federal government and extensively renovated, has been a tourist attraction just north of the Vancouver Barracks parade ground. This 1996 photo shows, at left, the Marshall House, headquarters of Army General George Marshall when he served at Vancouver in the 1930s.